101 REASONS TO VOTE FOR JOE BIDEN

Matthew Thomas Redmond

101 REASONS TO VOTE FOR JOE BIDEN
Matthew Thomas Redmond

ISBN: 978-1-7358303-2-2

Dedication

To the American Electorate

Table of Contents

Acknowledgements

I could write a multi-volume book filled with the names of those I'm thankful for. For brevity's sake I'll start by showing appreciation to my parents, Thomas Redmond and Roshanne Allen, and my siblings, Gabrielle, Benjamin, and Lexi whom I love. Thank you for your love and devotion to my endeavors and pursuits. The ideas to develop this book were developed over time from the many conversations I've had with family, friends, and colleagues, Tyler Edwards, Nick and Megan Unsworth, Steve Weatherford, Andy Friesella, and Ed Mylett. The long and sometimes late conversations with my college buddies Ricardo and Matt, my heated exchang with Morgan, and marathon chats with Camille, Talbott, Gabriella, Jana, and Rob. My dear friend Peter and Cousin Edward who both are on the far opposite side of the aisle from me, but whose genius I highly regard and seek out regularly. I am deeply grateful for these and many friendships I've nurtured over the years and those whose strength, advice, and wisdom I've drawn from for so long.

The exhaustive research for this book was thorough and far-reaching. Thanks to Hunter Estes, Sharif Ali, Mark Sutherland, Jase Burton, and Rob Arlett, all of whom helped shaped many of the ideas in this book.

To Mike Ficara, Eli Gonzalez, Meredith Cole, Andie Herrick, Jase Burton, Lee Spieckerman, and Cindy and William who took this book over the line. This team took my idea and ran warp speed to help me bring it to manifestation. I'm forever grateful and amazed at the incredible quality work and the compressed timeline you worked to, to help me to produce this work. Thank you for letting me get my message out to the masses.

And, to America, my home country and land that I love.

Introduction

There are times when I love politics. I love how it creates sub-communities of engaged and passionate people. I know of an older, retired woman—think of a grandmother and then add ten years to her—who took precious time out of her life to call more than 300,000 people in support of her candidate for President. She didn't do it for money or fame. She did it for the love she has based on her ideals of this country. Then there are the young people, far younger than me, still in high school or middle school who sign up for Civics classes and debate their ideologies because they want to make a difference. All across the country, others give up a year or more of their lives to become unpaid interns, with or without degrees or pedigrees, particularly during election years. Politics can bring out the best in people, and I love that.

On the other side of the coin, it can also bring out the worst in people. So, at times, I hate politics. It's become so divisive. The animosity in the air or on people's Facebook walls or Instagram feeds is nearly palpable. A few presidential terms ago, the average American simply voted based on their values and that was it. Those who were deeply into politics would have open dialogue and objective discourse. My, how times have changed!

As much as I'm involved in politics today, as evidenced by this book, I'm also fed up with it. The double standards employed by both parties are absolutely ridiculous. One side does something and the other side slams them, only to do the same thing a few months later, to be slammed by the side that did it first! And don't get me started with the media.

I guess the clinical diagnosis of my relationship with politics is that it's a love/hate relationship—and I'm okay with that. The important thing for me is to be involved and use my vote and my voice. My goal with my voice is to pull people out of the echo chamber (a metaphorical description of a situation in which beliefs are amplified or reinforced by repetitive communication inside a closed system that insulates people from rebuttal). My goal with my vote is to perform my civic duty by legally and publically standing with the side I trust most.

I wasn't born into politics, but it was all around me. I grew up in Baltimore, Maryland inside the DMV (Delaware/Maryland/Virginia) area, which by proximity is probably the most politically active region in the country. A single mother raised me, with help from her parents and pastors who owned a school in Baltimore city. The church and school made my grandparents civically active, because when I was growing up, the hot topic around politics was early childhood education, particularly in inner cities. It was common for me to see everyone run around to prepare for a politician who would come, along with members of the press, and give a speech or promise that money from the lottery would go to schools.

I've always loved America, the country I was born in. Always. I was born into a family of staunch patriots. One of my great uncles served as a Green Beret in the Vietnam War—he came back in a coffin. His body still lies, respectfully, in Arlington Cemetery. My other great uncle, Harry Blackwell Jr., also served in Vietnam, and also in Korea. Their service inspired me to serve. I also had two professors who poured a lot into me. One was a Brigadier General in the U.S. Army and the other was a Lieutenant Colonel in the U.S. Marine Corps. Those men helped shape my views of myself as a man and a citizen. But it wasn't until my late twenties that I decided I would join the military.

My mother had just departed on a flight from London to New York when the twin towers were attacked. The pilot gave the passengers the option of returning to London or flying to Canada, and they chose to return to London. But to me, to know that my mother was on a flight to New York when the towers were struck lit a fire in me to do my duty as a citizen and defend this country when I got older. As I write this book, I've been serving in the U.S. Army for three-and-a-half years, now in the National Guard part-time, while I run my trucking company and work as a banker for a nationwide bank. It's been an honor to give back to the country that has provided me with limitless opportunities.

What I enjoy most about politics today is the great, oftentimes spirited conversations (debates) I have with family members and friends whom I love and admire, regardless of how off-base I think they are. My cousin, Edward, is a big-time "Bernie" fan. On a personal note, I think he's a genius, the bleeding liberal part not withstanding. I was once asked to be interviewed so that I could be a subject matter expert for a book on politics, but I have so much respect for my cousin Eddy that I told the author to interview him instead. I also have a college buddy that I'm very close to who runs around yelling to defund the police. Having some arguments, but more respectful dialogue with them has taught me how to bridge the gap with people with opposing views. I enjoy the banter. And by talking to them, I began to learn how to better defend my position.

I'll admit, I have no idea how The Left thinks, but at least I'm willing to listen, and that's something most of this country needs to learn to do. I love being engaged. I'm not one to sit on the sidelines while the world goes up in flames. I am as up-to-date with current events as anyone, and I love explaining, defending, and protecting my conservative views. If people would only listen to reason... this world would be a better place.

I'm glad you chose to read this book. Please understand that I mean every word in it. I wrote it for several reasons. For one, I'm a proud, conservative, military-serving, law-abiding, entrepreneurial-minded, community-building, hard-working, black man who loves this country, and I support President Donald Trump whole-heartedly.

Secondly, I wrote it tongue-in-cheek style, so people can stop taking everything so seriously. At our core, we're all the same—we want to provide for our families (except for those who want the government to provide for their families), we all want to be safe (except for those who want to defund the police), we all want to grow healthy men and women (except for those who don't know if a boy is a boy or a girl is a girl), and we all want to use our talents in this capitalistic world and thrive (except for those who want socialism so that we're all the same). Wait. Maybe we're not the same after all. No, no... we are. Some people are just a little confused.

So, without any further ado... I've scoured Google, had plenty of conversations with people from The Left and The Right, analyzed many political debates, and I've heard the protestors. So, although Donald J. Trump gets my vote, hands down, here are 101 reasons I've found to vote for ~~Sleepy~~ Joe Biden.

101 Reasons to Vote for Joe Biden

Reason #1

Reason #2

Reason #3

Reason #4

Reason #5

Reason #6

Reason #7

Reason #8

Reason #9

Reason #10

Reason #11

Reason #12

Reason #13

Reason #14

Reason #15

Matthew Thomas Redmond

Reason #16

Reason #17

Reason #18

Reason #19

Reason #20

Reason #21

Reason #22

Reason #23

Reason #24

Reason #25

Reason #26

Reason #27

Reason #28

Reason #29

Reason #30

Reason #31

Reason #32

Reason #33

Reason #34

Reason #35

Reason #36

Reason #37

Reason #38

Reason #39

Reason #40

Reason #41

Reason #42

Reason #43

Reason #44

Reason #45

Reason #46

Reason #47

Reason #48

Reason #49

Reason #50

Reason #51

Reason #52

Reason #53

Reason #54

Reason #55

Reason #56

Reason #57

Reason #58

Reason #59

Reason #60

Reason #61

Reason #62

Reason #63

Reason #64

Reason #65

Reason #66

Reason #67

Reason #68

Reason #69

Reason #70

.

Reason #71

Reason #72

Reason #73

Reason #74

Reason #75

Reason #76

Reason #77

Reason #78

Reason #79

Reason #80

Reason #81

Reason #82

Reason #83

Reason #84

Reason #85

Reason #86

Reason #87

Reason #88

Reason #89

Reason #90

Reason #91

Reason #92

Reason #93

Reason #94

Reason #95

Reason #96

Reason #97

Reason #98

Reason #99

Reason #100

Reason #101

THE END

Epilogue: The Case for President Trump

Hopefully I've made a compelling argument of the reasons I believe there are to vote for Joe Biden...

On a serious note, my admiration for President Trump began decades before he entered politics, during my middle school years, when I came across his book in the local library, *The Art of the Deal.* After reading it, I was convinced that Trump was a shrewd, wise leader. What most inspired me was his self-confidence and persistence. After he took office, I had the opportunity to meet him. I looked him straight in the eyes and said, "America appreciates what you're doing."

There are many things I can say about President Trump and why re-electing him is crucial for our nation. Many people don't like his style or persona. But most of the Trump-haters and establishment Republican "Never Trumpers" actually despise him because he's been too effective at disrupting the odious order he inherited, an order that was so beneficial to the political and financial elites. They know that his commitment to "draining the swamp" will upend their livelihood, and they are scared.

Trump is accused of being racist because he lauds our law enforcement community and extolls law and order.

But, the truth is, the "Defund the Police" movement, which has been pushed by many Democrat donors and supporters, and only belatedly and tepidly criticized by Biden and Vice-Presidential candidate Kamala Harris, is the most racist policy in America. It would make life even more dangerous for black Americans living in our most distressed neighborhoods.

Of course, Harris herself excoriated Biden for his history on racial issues in a Democrat primary debate. In the 1970s, Biden said that integrating our schools would make them racial jungles, and that he wouldn't want his children to attend such schools.

The 1994 Clinton crime bill, which Biden ardently endorsed and helped pass, created the mass incarceration paradigm which locked-up countless black people for nonviolent— often petty—drug-related crimes. This destroyed black families and wreaked havoc on predominantly black communities that were already struggling.

It was Trump who, by enacting The First Step Act, was the first to begin unwinding this black mass incarceration. Already, thousands of black Americans have been released from prison under this law.

Education is the ladder out of the poverty pit. Yet, Biden has made it clear that he's a puppet of the public school teachers unions, expounding his desire to destroy charter schools and school choice for poor minority children. According to student performance metrics, these are the only schools that actually work for our least advantaged kids. So, Biden's policy would be a crime against our most vulnerable children, kids who weren't given the option at birth to select their zip code. Trump has championed school choice for poor minority children and promised to push it even more aggressively in a second term.

Biden would literally be the worst president for black Americans imaginable.

President Trump has a proven track record of relentlessly fighting for middle-class American workers. He was sounding the alarm about other nations taking advantage of our country on trade and stealing our jobs as far back as the 1980s, when Japan was our biggest threat (and still runs a huge trade surplus with the U.S.). China put the Japanese trade scheme on steroids, sucking literally millions of well-paying manufacturing jobs out of our country. This was particularly devastating for African-American workers in northern industrial centers like Chicago, Detroit, Cleveland, and Pittsburgh. Much of the inner-city decay and violence we see today can be traced to the horrific trade deals that enabled China, Japan, Mexico, and Germany to hollow out America's industrial base. During his decades in the U.S. Senate, Biden strongly supported every terrible trade treaty and heartily endorsed China's admittance into the World Trade Organization, which gave it unfettered access to the rich U.S. market but didn't prevent it from protecting its market from imports, impairing the ability of American companies to do business in that country and subsidizing its export-driven industries.

Once Biden was sworn in as Vice-President, China solidified its hold on him by enabling his son Hunter, who'd been discharged from the military for drug use, to amass millions of dollars from Chinese communist party-backed firms. This is on top of the enormous sums paid to Hunter Biden by the corrupt Ukraine natural gas company Burisma. How can

Biden possibly be tough on China given his son's financial connections to its authoritarian regime?

Trump totally upended the disastrous trade regime put in place over many decades by the political lackeys of Wall Street fat cats like Biden. He imposed heavy import tariffs on Chinese goods, which reduced our massive trade deficit with that predatory country by 20% while generating tens of billions of dollars in new revenue for the federal government. Trump canceled the horrific NAFTA trade deal with Mexico and Canada and quickly negotiated and got the Senate to ratify the far more U.S. worker-friendly United States-Mexico-Canada Agreement (USMCA).

Simultaneously, Trump enacted the most dramatic tax cut and reform since Ronald Reagan was in office. This gave a huge tax break to middle-class families and small businesses, and provided unprecedented incentives for investment in economically-struggling, predominantly minority, inner cities.

These dramatic trade and tax policies quickly bore fruit. Before the COVID pandemic, our economy added millions of jobs, including over half-a-million manufacturing jobs. We achieved the lowest unemployment rate in modern history, not only overall, but for black Americans, Latino Americans, and women. Middle-class Americans experienced the highest growth in real income in decades.

Of course, the COVID pandemic—which President Trump accurately refers to as the China Virus—took a terrible toll on our country in lives and had a devastating impact on our economy. Once the COVID scourge became apparent, Biden again showed his predilection for China by excoriating the president for his China travel ban—even though it saved hundreds of thousands of American lives.

Those on the Left who accuse President Trump of valuing money over lives fail to explain why he led a virtual shutdown of the booming economy he was presiding over. And, while the Woodward book tapes capture the president saying he "played down" the pandemic to prevent a panic, Trump also marshaled the most massive mobilization of our military, private sector, and public health infrastructure since World War II. The U.S. leads the world in COVID testing by a wide margin. Despite our large elderly population and much higher rate of obesity and diabetes, we have a lower per-capita COVID death rate than almost every large European nation (many of which have the vaunted socialized healthcare systems extolled by Bernie Sanders and now the Biden/Harris ticket).

Due to President Trump's Operation Warp Speed, multiple COVID vaccines are in Phase III clinical trials, with at least one almost certain to be ready for distribution before the end of the year. This is the most rapid timeline for a novel virus vaccine in history. Nationally, COVID cases are down 40%. Deaths are down 85%. Over 98% of those infected with the virus now recover.

Contrary to the destructive austerity which has been integral to Republican economic orthodoxy, President Trump's COVID-19 economic rescue package was the most massive economic relief program in our country's history, much larger in relative terms than either FDR's New Deal or the Obama/Biden Great Recession "Stimulus." As a result, we've already regained three million of the jobs lost due to COVID. The unemployment rate has fallen dramatically to 8%, far lower than economists' projections. As of this writing, we're on track for a barn-burning third quarter growth rate. Home sales are off-the-charts. Meanwhile, Biden has blithely said that he's willing to again shut down our economy if nameless "scientists" say he should.

I'm also alarmed by Joe Biden's awful track record on foreign policy and national security. In his memoir, *Duty*, venerated former Obama Secretary of Defense Robert Gates wrote of Biden, "I think he has been wrong on nearly every major foreign policy and national security issue over the past four decades." Biden, according to Gates, said that "when the Shah fell in Iran in 1979, that was a step forward for progress toward human rights in Iran. He opposed virtually every element of President Reagan's defense build-up. He voted against the first Gulf War. So, on a number of these major issues, I just frankly, over a long period of time, felt that he had been wrong."

In subsequent interviews, Gates said he stood by those words. He also wrote that, as VP, Biden was "poisoning the well" against the military leadership and that "suspicion and distrust of senior military officers by senior White House officials—including the President and Vice-President—became a big problem for me."

I couldn't unread what I read about the former vice president from Gates, a man who's worked under presidents of both political parties and is highly respected on both sides of the aisle. To me, this reinforces my serious doubts about Biden's ability to serve as Commander-in-Chief.

Perhaps nothing President Trump has achieved is more noteworthy than his remake of the federal judiciary. Two Trump-appointed justices sit on the Supreme Court, and he's just appointed a third, Amy Coney Barrett, a brilliant constitutionalist who's almost certain to be confirmed. President Trump has also appointed a record number of federal appellate court judges. In an era when the Left relies on the courts to impose a radical agenda that would be unachievable through legislation, the enduring impact of Trump's judicial appointments cannot be overstated.

I've seen many parents of modest, humble means raise children who turn out stellar. And, too often, I've seen affluent parents who shower their children cash and opportunities only to see them squander those blessings and fail as adults. While the Left and Hollywood elites incessantly mock and malign President Trump's adult children, any objective assessment of their careers shows that they've been hardworking and highly effective. President Trump raised his children with this principle: No Drugs, No Alcohol, and No Cigarettes! And anyone who's seen Donald Jr., Eric, Ivanka, or Tiffany speak on television can't deny that they're engaging, eloquent, and poised. That certainly doesn't happen by accident—it takes strong parenting.

The Trump kids clearly revere and respect their father and demonstrate that the offspring of the highly affluent can build on their legacy by achieving success in their own right. Perhaps this is what the Left and Trump-haters fear most, that the President's impressive progeny will create a Kennedy-like political dynasty.

The political elites, the donor class, the lobbyists, the establishment politicians of both parties, loathe President Trump. Not because of his Tweets, not because of his bombast, but because he's kept his promises. Trump *is* draining the DC swamp. He's ending the endless wars and he's refusing to kowtow to the Military-Industrial Complex. He's making America's middle-class workers—not CEOs and hedge fund titans—our first priority.

Meanwhile, the radical Left, bolstered by huge donations from George Soros and other billionaires willing to tear our country asunder so that they can reconstruct it in a manner to their liking, are determined to destroy Trump because they know he's the only political force formidable enough to stop them.

With the sole exception of Fox News, every big media outlet—and the vast majority of big media reporters and correspondents—have abandoned the journalistic norms of objectivity and detachment in order to take down a president that they claim has abandoned the norms of his office.

With so many powerful actors arrayed against him, President Trump's only hope of remaining in office, forestalling the Leftist onslaught and fulfilling his pro-American agenda, is his army of supporters. The question is, will they stand behind him in sufficient numbers in this election? Will Democrat-controlled states and cities ensure that all of their votes are counted, and that Trump votes aren't diluted by fraudulent ones?

Winning. Now it's up to us.

About the Author

Matthew Thomas Redmond was born to Thomas Redmond and Roshane Allen in April 1990. He holds a BA from Georgetown University. Following in the footsteps of two of his great uncles, Harry Jr., and Frederic Delano Blackwell, he currently serves in the United States Army National Guard.

His consumption of politics began in his middle school years. This was a time in American history where 9/11 happened, people were debating whether or not we should go to war with Iraq, the was an economic crash, and of government bail-outs.

He considers himself a patriot and is a staunch, unapologetic conservative. He conducts virtual and live summits where he brings people together to intelligently and rationally "debate" all of the most divisive issues of our times. Matthew is a sought-after speaker who lends his voice and his vote to Keep America Great.

When he's not helping save the world from socialism and anarchy, he can be seen fishing or skiing, depending on the season. He's an avid reader and loves to spend time with family and friends.

To book Matthew Thomas Redmond as a speaker for an event or to be a guest on a podcast or show or as a subject matter expert, follow him on Twitter @matthewredmond, and at www.matthewredmond.com

Lightning Source UK Ltd.
Milton Keynes UK
UKHW020249221120
373825UK00010B/608